Credits

Author

Abhimanyu Kumar Vatsa

Reviewer

Ahsan Murshed

Acquisition Editor

Akram Hussain

Commissioning Editor

Shreerang Deshpande

Technical Editor

Nitee Shetty

Project Coordinator

Siddhant Shetty

Proofreader

Maria Gould

Production Coordinator

Prachali Bhiwandkar

Cover Work

Prachali Bhiwandkar

Cover Image

Sheetal Aute

About the Author

Abhimanyu Kumar Vatsa works at Coxtan College, located in Bokaro Steel City, India as a lecturer focused on web technologies. He is a Microsoft MVP in ASP.NET/IIS. He loves to blog and started blogging in June 2009. He holds a bachelor's degree in Computer Science and Applications, a master's degree in Information Technology, and a few application-level diplomas. He moved to Bokaro Steel City from a remote village to pursue higher education in March 2003, and that was when he saw a computer with Windows 95 OS on Pentium 1 for the first time, and since then, he has never looked back.

A big thank you to my mom, dad, my sister Ambuj, my brother Avnish, the Indian MVP Community, and to you for reading this book. Enjoy!

About the Reviewer

Ahsan Murshed is an ex-MVP (Microsoft Most Valuable Professional) for the period of 2011-2013. Now he is working as a software engineer, with more than 6 years of experience in the design, prototyping, development, and deployment of various scales of business solutions. He is interested in working on large scale business applications such as MS SharePoint, MS Dynamics CRM, and so on.

I would like to dedicate this book to my family, my parents, wife, and Ayesha, and also to my friends who give me tremendous support. Thank you friends for all your support.

www.PacktPub.com

Support files, eBooks, discount offers and more

You might want to visit www.PacktPub.com for support files and downloads related to your book.

Did you know that Packt offers eBook versions of every book published, with PDF and ePub files available? You can upgrade to the eBook version at www.PacktPub.com and as a print book customer, you are entitled to a discount on the eBook copy. Get in touch with us at service@packtpub.com for more details.

At www.PacktPub.com, you can also read a collection of free technical articles, sign up for a range of free newsletters and receive exclusive discounts and offers on Packt books and eBooks.

http://PacktLib.PacktPub.com

Do you need instant solutions to your IT questions? PacktLib is Packt's online digital book library. Here, you can access, read and search across Packt's entire library of books.

Why Subscribe?

- ▶ Fully searchable across every book published by Packt
- ▶ Copy and paste, print and bookmark content
- ▶ On demand and accessible via web browser

Free Access for Packt account holders

If you have an account with Packt at www.PacktPub.com, you can use this to access PacktLib today and view nine entirely free books. Simply use your login credentials for immediate access.

Table of Contents

Preface

Welcome to *Instant Razor View Engine How-to*. This book will take you on a journey through using the Razor view engine in MVC applications. In the very beginning of the book, we will learn why this technology is useful by comparing with other view engines, and as you progress you will learn inline codes, block codes, mixed codes, conditional and repetitive statements, layouts and nested layouts, directives, scaffolding, models, directives, helpers with extension and declarative, partial views, and much more about Razor with some really unique examples.

You will find this book a vital companion as you progress through your reading. So let this Razor journey begin!

What this book covers

Creating the project (Should know) helps you learn how to get a project ready to start writing Razor syntaxes.

Fundamental Razor syntaxes (Must know) shows you the syntactic differences between Razor and ASPX view engines. You will also learn about inline code expressions, code block expressions, mixed code expressions, conditional statements, loops, comments, text tags, language parsers, and much more.

Razor layout pages (Become an expert) helps you learn about all the concepts of layout pages, nested layout pages, RenderBody, RenderSection, and much more in detail.

Models in Razor (Must know) helps you learn the concept of models, scaffolding views, directives, and much more.

Razor helpers (Must know) talks about helpers with extension methods, declarative syntax, and standard helpers.

Partial views (Should know) explores partial views including Partial helpers, RenderPartial helpers, Action helpers, RenderAction helpers, and much more.

What you need for this book

The minimum requirement for programming with Razor syntax is Visual Studio 2010 or Visual Web Developer 2010. These versions will offer you the promised IntelliSense support. However, I will recommend you to download the latest available version of Visual Studio 2012 or Visual Web Developer 2012 from the Microsoft website (http://www.microsoft.com/). So, whatever Visual Studio version you use, we need MVC 3 or MVC 4 project templates or WebMatrix.

Who this book is for

This book is for any developer who uses .NET/MVC3/MVC4/WebMatrix and would benefit from learning the new syntax. Being a developer, I understand all the pain we can experience with web applications. We always look for alternatives that can make our coding life easier and the people at Microsoft are working hard to make it possible. If you are also looking for alternatives, simply start learning Razor.

Conventions

In this book, you will find a number of styles of text that distinguish between different kinds of information. Here are some examples of these styles, and an explanation of their meaning.

Code words in text are shown as follows: "The `Edit` action method is linked to the `Edit.cshtml` view file."

A block of code is set as follows:

```
public ActionResult Index()
{
    ViewBag.Message = "Razor View Engine";
    return View();
}
```

New terms and **important words** are shown in bold. Words that you see on the screen, in menus or dialog boxes for example, appear in the text like this: "Select the **Empty MVC controller** template and click on **Add**."

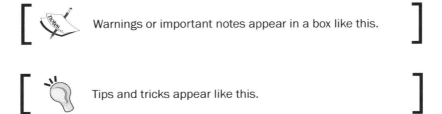

Warnings or important notes appear in a box like this.

Tips and tricks appear like this.

Reader feedback

Feedback from our readers is always welcome. Let us know what you think about this book—what you liked or may have disliked. Reader feedback is important for us to develop titles that you really get the most out of.

To send us general feedback, simply send an e-mail to feedback@packtpub.com, and mention the book title via the subject of your message.

If there is a topic that you have expertise in and you are interested in either writing or contributing to a book, see our author guide on www.packtpub.com/authors.

Customer support

Now that you are the proud owner of a Packt book, we have a number of things to help you to get the most from your purchase.

Errata

Although we have taken every care to ensure the accuracy of our content, mistakes do happen. If you find a mistake in one of our books—maybe a mistake in the text or the code—we would be grateful if you would report this to us. By doing so, you can save other readers from frustration and help us improve subsequent versions of this book. If you find any errata, please report them by visiting http://www.packtpub.com/submit-errata, selecting your book, clicking on the **errata submission form** link, and entering the details of your errata. Once your errata are verified, your submission will be accepted and the errata will be uploaded on our website, or added to any list of existing errata, under the Errata section of that title. Any existing errata can be viewed by selecting your title from http://www.packtpub.com/support.

Piracy

Piracy of copyright material on the Internet is an ongoing problem across all media. At Packt, we take the protection of our copyright and licenses very seriously. If you come across any illegal copies of our works, in any form, on the Internet, please provide us with the location address or website name immediately so that we can pursue a remedy.

Please contact us at copyright@packtpub.com with a link to the suspected pirated material.

We appreciate your help in protecting our authors, and our ability to bring you valuable content.

Questions

You can contact us at questions@packtpub.com if you are having a problem with any aspect of the book, and we will do our best to address it.

Instant Razor View Engine How-to

Welcome to *Instant Razor View Engine How-to*, where we take you on a journey through using the Razor view engine in MVC applications. Even if you wish to use Microsoft WebMatrix tools with Razor, this book will help you.

Introduction

Let's quickly start by looking at what MVC architecture is and how it is different from Web Forms.

The **Model-View-Controller** (**MVC**) pattern is an architectural design principle that separates the components of a web application. This separation gives more control over the individual parts of the application, which lets us develop, modify, and test them easier. MVC is part of the ASP.NET framework. Developing an MVC application is an alternative to developing ASP.NET Web Forms pages; it does not replace the Web Forms model.

ASP.NET MVC comes with two view engines by default; ASPX (also known as Web Forms view engine) and Razor. The view engine is responsible for creating HTML from our views. Views are usually a mixture of HTML and a programming language. The Razor view engine was introduced as part of MVC 3 and the Microsoft WebMatrix toolset.

Razor is not a new language; it is the response to one of the most requested suggestions received by the MVC team to provide a clean, lightweight, quicker, and friendlier view engine that minimizes the number of characters and keystrokes required in a file and enables a fast and fluid coding workflow.

If you select Visual Basic as your programming language, when you add a new view in your project, you will be offered to select either **ASPX (VB)** or **Razor (VBHTML)** view engines, as shown in the following screenshot:

If you select Visual C# as your programming language, when you add a new view in your project, you will be offered to select either **ASPX(C#)** or **Razor (CSHTML)** view engines, as shown in the following screenshot:

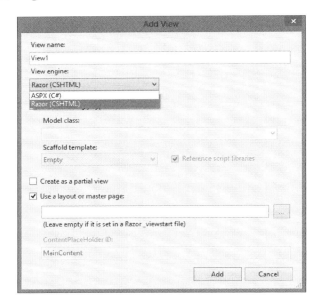

The ASPX view engine can have either a `.aspx` or `.ascx` (user control) file extension, and the Razor view engine can have either a `.cshtml` (for C#) or `.vbhtml` (for VB) file extension; this depends on what programming language you have selected for your project. One of the things that you will love is the choice and flexibility for view engine selection while adding the view. You can use different view engines in the same project/application; it is all up to you.

Other popular view engines used today are **Spark** and **NHaml** (pronounced "enamel"); these are pluggable view engines in MVC.

Why Razor?

In short, using Razor is rather wrapping your code elements in view with `<%  %>` tags, for which you can simply use an `@` symbol. Actually, the Razor view engine has syntactic awareness built into it, thus there is no need to close your tags. If you want to declare multiple lines of code you can wrap your code in the following symbols `@{code goes here}`. This will go a long way to reduce the tag soup that you get in your views.

Versions

When the Razor view engine was introduced with MVC 3 in January 2011, it was Version 1. The latest version of Razor is v2, which was released with ASP.NET MVC 4. Razor v2 includes a bunch of new features that we will cover throughout this book.

Prerequisites

The minimum requirement to program with Razor syntax is Visual Studio 2010 or Visual Web Developer 2010. These versions will offer you the promised IntelliSense support. However, I will recommend you to download the latest version available. As of now, the latest version is Visual Studio 2012 or Visual Web Developer 2012 available from the Microsoft website. So, whatever Visual Studio version you use, you need to have MVC 3 or MVC 4 project templates.

Creating the project (Should know)

In this recipe, we will go and look at the available project templates for ASP.NET MVC 4 Web Application. Then, we will take you through a step-by-step approach to create and run ASP.NET MVC 4 Web Application. At the end, we will write some quick Razor syntax for testing.

Getting ready

Before getting started with Razor coding we need a project allowing the use of Razor syntaxes. The Razor view engine is the default view engine for MVC projects; however, we can use Razor syntaxes in Web Forms projects by installing its binaries. Mixing ASPX and Razor syntaxes on the same page is officially not supported, the reason being both syntaxes are developed for different goals, so we need to have a separate view page for Razor syntaxes.

How to do it...

Now, let's go ahead and learn how to set up an MVC Web Application project to use Razor syntaxes discussed throughout this book.

This is going to be a step-by-step task to set up the project, so follow these steps:

1. Start Visual Studio or Visual Web Developer.

2. In the **File** menu, click on **New | Project**.

3. In the **New Project** dialog box, select **Visual C#** as the programming language and then **ASP.NET MVC 4 Web Application**.

4. Finish this by clicking on **OK**.

5. Now the following dialog box appears, in which you need to select the **Project Template**:

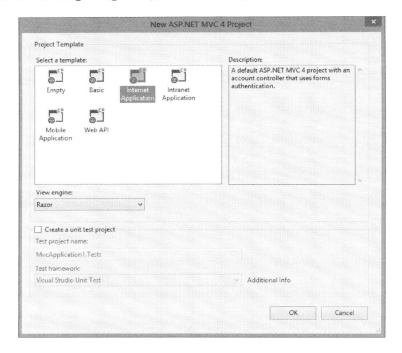

6. The **Internet Application** template is a regular template for any MVC web application project. This template comes with pre-packed required libraries that help us to build applications to perform CRUD operations on the fly.

7. The preceding screenshot shows the minimum number of available templates released with Visual Studio 2012; this may vary depending upon the update/version you running. For example, I have installed ASP.NET Web Tools 2012.2 Update on another computer and now I have **Single Page Application** (also known as **SPA**) and **Facebook Application** templates. You could have more templates depending upon the updates you have installed.

8. In the preceding dialog box, you can also see an option to select **View engine**. Select the **Razor** view engine here and don't worry, you will have the opportunity to select the view engine each time you add a new view page in an application.

9. Finish by clicking on **OK**.

10. Now, you will have a ready-to-run project on your screen, like the one shown in the following screenshot:

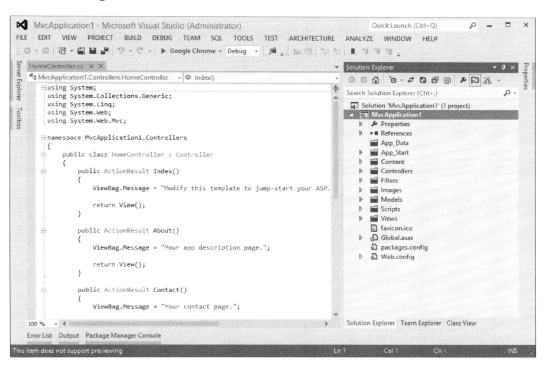

At this time if you run this application, the MVC runtime will render the `Index` view of `Home` controller by default. We can control this by adding or modifying the route values which can be found in the `RouteConfig.cs` file inside the `App_Start` folder, as follows:

```
public class RouteConfig
{
    public static void RegisterRoutes(RouteCollection routes)
    {
        routes.IgnoreRoute("{resource}.axd/{*pathInfo}");

        routes.MapRoute(
            name: "Default",
            url: "{controller}/{action}/{id}",
            defaults: new { controller = "Home", action = "Index", id = UrlParameter.Optional }
        );
    }
}
```

Now, let's try running this application; you will have following output:

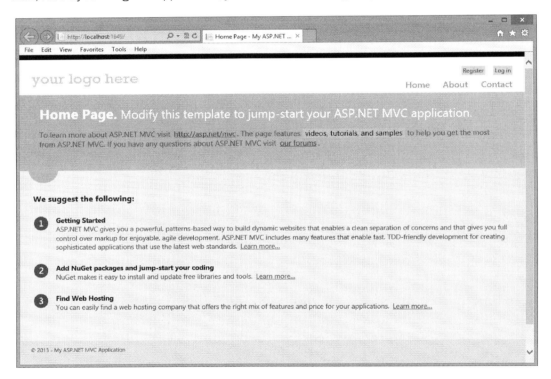

If you look at the `Index.cshtml` code (given in the following screenshot), you will notice how quickly (with a small amount of code) the code generated the preceding output. That's the power of Razor.

```
Index.cshtml  ⊕ ×
    @{
        ViewBag.Title = "Home Page";
    }
    @section featured {
        <section class="featured">
            <div class="content-wrapper">
                <hgroup class="title">
                    <h1>@ViewBag.Title.</h1>
                    <h2>@ViewBag.Message</h2>
                </hgroup>
                <p>
                    To learn more about ASP.NET MVC visit
                    <a href="http://asp.net/mvc" title="ASP.NET MVC Website">http://asp.net/mvc</a>.
                    The page features <mark>videos, tutorials, and samples</mark> to help you get the most from ASP.NET MVC.
                    If you have any questions about ASP.NET MVC visit
                    <a href="http://forums.asp.net/1146.aspx/1?MVC" title="ASP.NET MVC Forum">our forums</a>.
                </p>
            </div>
        </section>
    }
    <h3>We suggest the following:</h3>
```

Look at the highlighted codes; these are the Razor syntaxes. At the top, we have a Razor code block and then a section (you will learn about it later) by the name `featured` and inside the section we have two `ViewBag`.

ViewBag uses the dynamic feature that was added in C# 4.0. We can say that `ViewBag` is a combination of `ViewData` and a dynamic wrapper around the `ViewData` dictionary.

ViewData and **ViewBag** serve the same purpose in allowing developers to pass data from controllers to views. When you put objects in either one of these, the objects become accessible in the view.

TempData allows us to store data that will survive for a redirect only. After redirecting, the stored data is automatically evicted.

We are going to learn Razor syntax throughout this book, so I'll recommend adding a clean new controller and view where we will write our codes.

This will be a step-by-step task to add a controller and a view, so follow these steps:

1. Right-click on the `Controllers` folder and add a new controller.

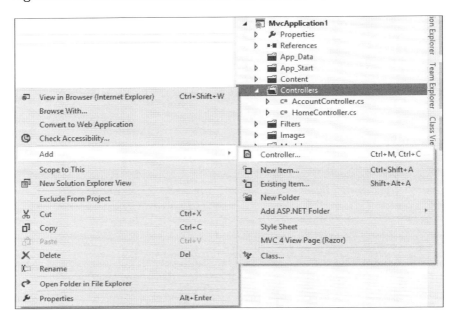

2. In the appeared dialog box, change the controller name to `Demo`, select the **Empty MVC controller** template, and click on **Add**.

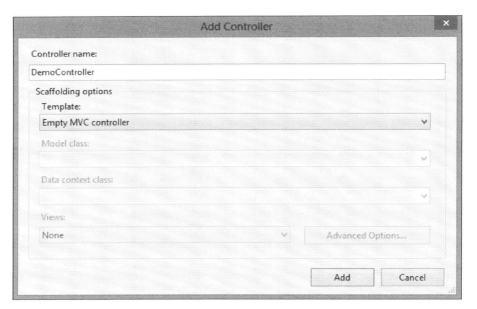

3. Now, you will have a controller named `Demo` with an `Index` method. You just add a `ViewBag.Message` property inside the `Index` method that will return the view page. After adding `ViewBag.Message` to your code, it should look as follows:

```
public ActionResult Index()
{
    ViewBag.Message = "Razor View Engine";
    return View();
}
```

4. To add a view page for the `Index` method, right-click on the **Index()** method and click on **Add View...**:

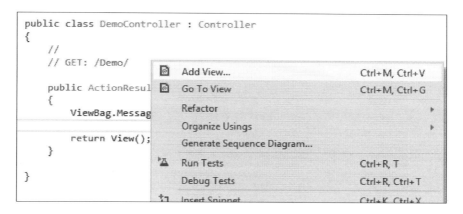

5. Now, in the appeared window, select **View name** as **Index** and **View engine** as **Razor (CSHTML)**. Leave the rest as it is and click on **Add**.

6. You will have an **Index.cshtml** page inside **Views | Demo** in the project root. Look at the following screenshot:

MVC follows the **Convention over Configuration** concept, which is one of the most distinguishing features. Rather than saving all the settings in the configuration files, MVC heavily relies on the common agreement (convention) such as folder structures and naming conventions.

When we create an MVC project using any MVC project templates, you will see the common structure of folders and files. The structure of files and folders is not just for your convenience. It follows the predefined rules. Thus the developers should understand well how folders and files are organized. Refer to the following points for a few examples:

> ▶ Controller classes must have names that end with Controller such as HomeController.

> ▶ Views and partial views should go into the `/Views/Controllername'` and `'/Views/Shared` folders respectively.

> ▶ The default view for an action method should be named after that method. For example, the `Edit` action method is linked to the `Edit.cshtml` view file.

> ▶ The naming convention for layouts is to prefix the file with an underscore (_) character and the layout files are placed in the `/Views/Shared` folder.

To run this newly added view page, **Index.cshtml**, you need to browse to `http://localhost:port/demo` where `demo` is the controller and by default MVC maps the `Index.cshtml` view. Now, this page will allow the use of Razor syntax with C# language.

Let's go ahead and follow the same steps given earlier and use the ASPX view engine instead of Razor. Also, add a `Demo` controller, `Index` action method, and a view page, `Index.aspx`. It will look like the following:

```
Index.aspx    DemoController.cs
    <%@ Page Title="" Language="C#" MasterPageFile="~/Views/Shared/Site.Master" Inherits="System.Web.Mvc.ViewPage<dynamic>" %>

<asp:Content ID="Content1" ContentPlaceHolderID="TitleContent" runat="server">
    Index
</asp:Content>

<asp:Content ID="Content2" ContentPlaceHolderID="MainContent" runat="server">

    <h2>Index</h2>

</asp:Content>

<asp:Content ID="Content3" ContentPlaceHolderID="FeaturedContent" runat="server">
</asp:Content>

<asp:Content ID="Content4" ContentPlaceHolderID="ScriptsSection" runat="server">
</asp:Content>
```

Now, compare both view pages; `Index.cshtml`, which is generated by the Razor view engine; and `Index.aspx`, which is generated by the ASPX view engine. Can you see the amount of code in both views?

To give you another example, I would like to show you the syntactic differences between the Razor view engine and the ASPX view engine by putting images of both the view engines together. I used a `<p>` tag to display a line and a `<div>` tag that will contain an unordered list generated by a `for` loop.

Let me take this opportunity to ask you, which one would you prefer in development? Take a look at the screenshot of both view engines:

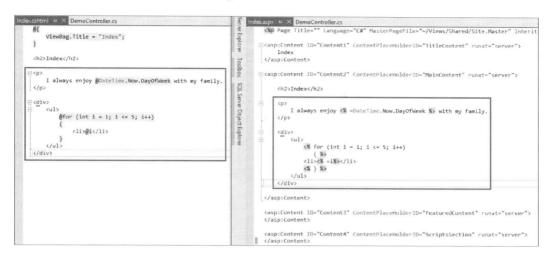

Here, you may not be able to understand some points, but don't worry; we will cover everything later. If you look at the preceding screenshot and compare, you will find:

- To print a day of a week, I have to use `<% =DateTime.Now.DayOfWeek %>` on the ASPX view page whereas just use `@DateTime.Now.DayOfWeek` on the Razor view page.

- To print a 1 to 5 table using a `for` loop, I have to use the following code snippet on ASPX view page:

```
<%for (int i = 1; i <= 5; i++)
    { %>
<li><% =i%></li>
<% } %>
```

whereas just the following code on the Razor view page:

```
@for (int i = 1; i <= 5; i++)
{
<li>@i</li>
}
```

- Now tell me, isn't this painful in the ASPX view page, switching C# to HTML and then HTML to C# again?

> ▸ You will also notice the difference in the code quantity of both the view engines produces the following output:

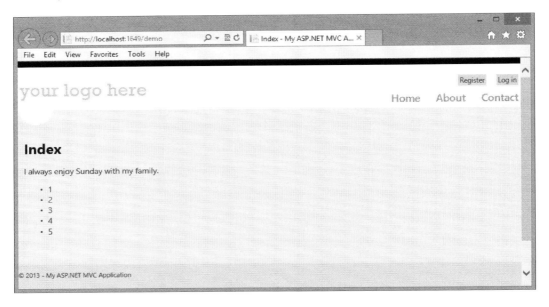

We are using the C# programming language the with Razor and ASPX view engines. We can also make use of the VB programming language with the Razor and ASPX view engines, as shown in the following screenshot:

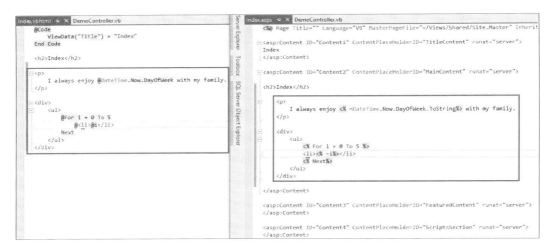

Thus we can say that Razor looks beautiful with VB as well. So, with the help of @, the magical character, we can make our job quick and simple.

There's more...

In this recipe, to use the Razor syntax we only set up the project using the MVC Internet Application template; however, you can also use any other template such as Empty, Basic, and Intranet—it is totally up to you, just remember to pick the Razor view engine whenever prompted. Also, Razor syntax can be used with the WebMatrix tools, so reading this book will help you with developing applications using Razor.

In this recipe, we quickly jumped by looking at the MVC architecture overview. If you want to read more visit `http://goo.gl/bL2Pw`.

Fundamental Razor syntaxes (Must know)

In this recipe we will go and look at inline, code block and mixed expressions; and some fundamental Razor syntaxes such as conditional statements, loops, and comments.

Getting ready

In the *Creating the project (Should know)* recipe, we created a project using the **Internet Application** template with the Razor view engine and added a `Demo` controller and an `Index.cshtml` view page. In this view page you can try all the Razor syntaxes given in this recipe.

How to do it...

Here, let's start learning the fundamental Razor syntaxes. All Razor syntaxes can be written using three different approaches: inline, code block, and mixed.

Inline code expressions

Inline code expressions are always written in a single line, as follows:

```
I always enjoy @DateTime.Now.DayOfWeek with my family.
```

At runtime, the inline code expression, which is `@DateTime.Now.DayOfWeek`, will be converted into a day, such as Sunday. This can be seen in the following screenshot:

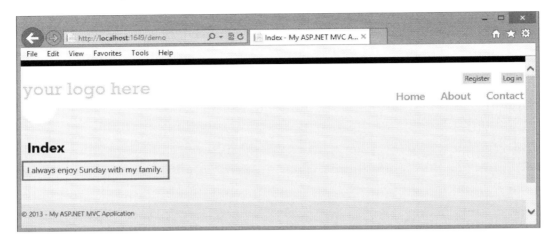

Let's look at one more example, which will pass the controller's `ViewBag` and `ViewData` messages on the view.

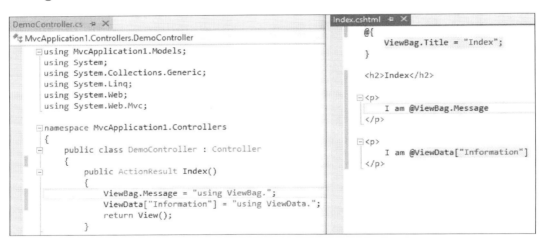

The rendered output will be as follows:

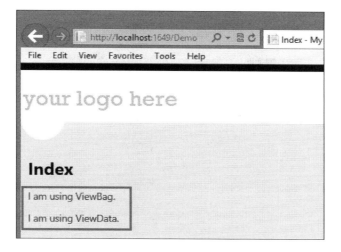

Code block expression

Code block expression is actually a set of multiple code lines that start and end with @{ }. The use of opening (@{) and closing (}) characters is mandatory, even for single line of C# or VB code; as shown in the following screenshot:

```
Index.cshtml
    @{
        ViewBag.Title = "Index";
    }

    <h2>Index</h2>

    <p>
        @{
            var user = "Abhimanyu K Vatsa";
            var today = DateTime.Now.Date;
        }

        Welcome back <b>@user</b> on @today
    </p>
```

This will render the following output:

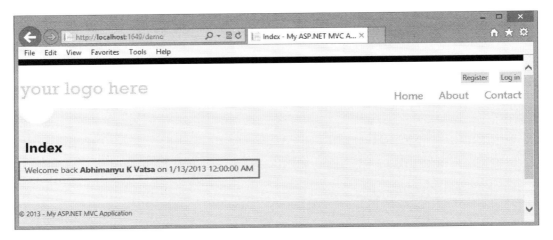

Mixed code expression

Mixed code expression is a set of multiple inline code expressions in a code block where we switch between C# and HTML. The magical key here is @:, which allows writing HTML in a code block, as follows:

```
@{
    ViewBag.Title = "Index";
}

<h2>Index</h2>

<p>
    @{
        var user = "Abhimanyu K Vatsa";
        var today = DateTime.Now.Date;

        @:Welcome back <b>@user</b> on @today
    }
</p>
```

This will render the following output:

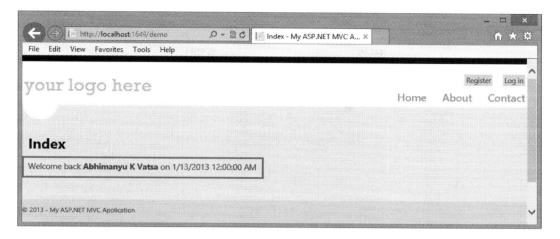

So, this is all about how we write the code on Razor view page. You learned all these three approaches with examples, let's move on now.

We can see the conditional statements (also known as conditional expressions) being in programming languages such as C#, VB, C, C++, and Java. The good part is that Razor supports writing conditional statements, let's learn them all. I am not going to discuss what all these conditional statements can do or what are the differences, I'll just show you a quick example on each of them:

> ▶ The `if` statement

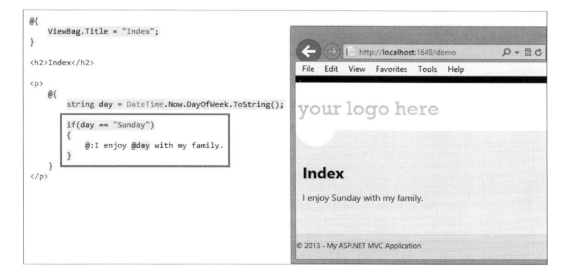

In the preceding screenshot, I wrapped every code inside a single code block expression that starts and ends with @{ }. So, when one uses this syntax, there is no need to use an @ before the `if` condition, as the following example:

```
<p>
    @{
        string day = DateTime.Now.DayOfWeek.ToString();
    }
    @if(day == "Sunday")
    {
        @:I enjoy @day with my family.
    }
</p>
```

▶ The `if-else` statement

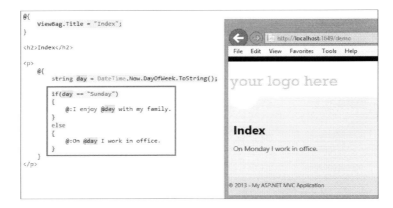

▶ The `if-else if-else` statement

```
@{
    ViewBag.Title = "Index";
}

<h2>Index</h2>

<p>
    @{
        string day = DateTime.Now.DayOfWeek.ToString();
        if(day == "Sunday")
        {
            @:I enjoy @day with my family.
        }
        else if(day == "Monday")
        {
            @:On @day I work in office.
        }
        else
        {
            @:On @day I work in Bokaro Steel Plant.
        }
    }
</p>
```

That's all you need to know about the simple conditional statements. Try it out yourself, it works great. You will feel like writing C# conditional statements all day.

We can also use ternary operators in Razor. If you have a condition that can be checked as an `if` situation with one alternate `else`, you can use the ternary operator that is a combination of `?` and `:` characters. Here is an example showing the use of ternary operators:

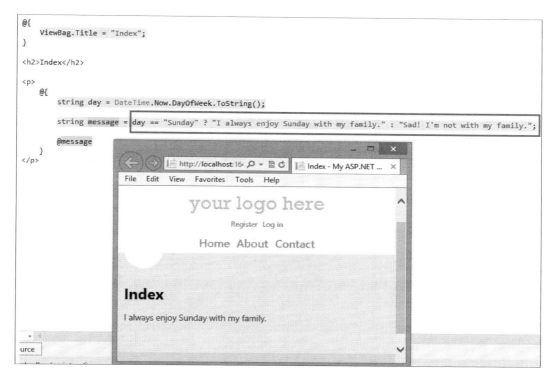

I think things are much clear to you now that you know how to write conditional statements using Razor syntax. Let's go ahead and learn looping in Razor.

Looping is another essential ability to repeat a block of code a defined number of times. In C#, they come in different variants and Razor supports all; let's look at a few examples.

▶ The `for` loop

The `for` loop is a bit different. It's better when you know how many iterations you want, either because you know the exact amount of iterations, or because you have a variable containing the amount.

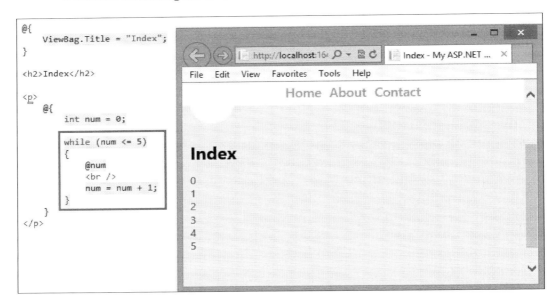

▶ The `foreach` loop

The `foreach` loop operates on collections of items, for instance, list/array or another built-in collection type.

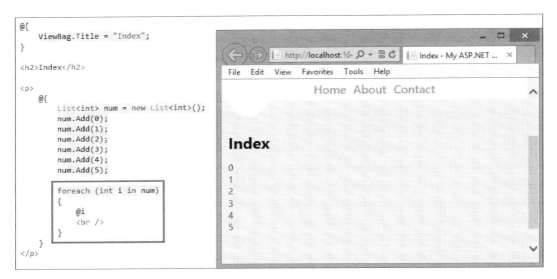

In preceeding loop example, I have used code block expressions, however, this can be done using inline code expression also, as follows:

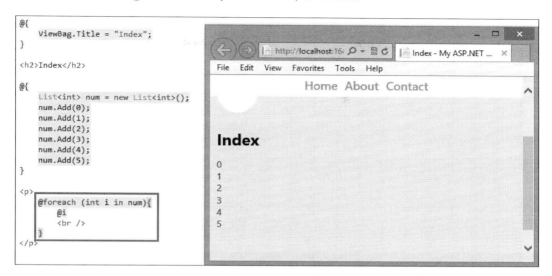

▶ The `while` loop

The `while` loop simply executes a block of code as long as the condition you give it is `true`.

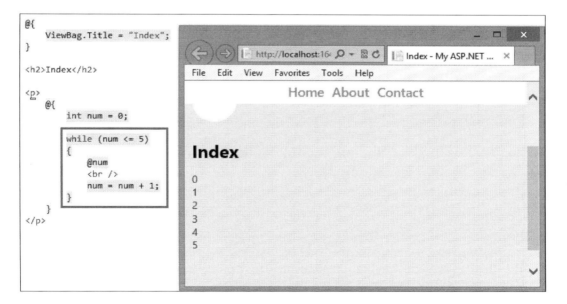

▸ The `dowhile` loop

The `dowhile` loop evaluates the condition after the loop has executed, which makes sure that the code block is always executed at least once.

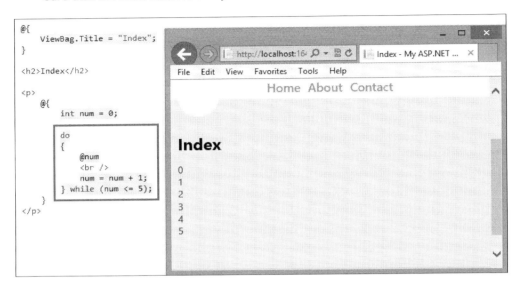

So, that's all you need to know about looping using Razor syntaxes. Now you understand how simple Razor syntax is, keep reading.

Unlike C# and VB, we can also comment the Razor syntax, which is also essential to learn. Let's learn them.

The comments in Razor are always delimited by `@*` and `*@`. This can be seen in the following screenshot:

```
@{
    ViewBag.Title = "Index";
}

<h2>Index</h2>

@*

<p>
    @{
        string user = "Abhimanyu K Vatsa";
        @user
    }
</p>

*@
```

If you are inside a code block, you can also use `//` and `/* */` comment delimiters, shown as follows:

```
@{
    ViewBag.Title = "Index";
}

<h2>Index</h2>

<p>
    @{
        //string user = "Abhimanyu K Vatsa";

        /*
        @user
        */
    }
</p>
```

That's all about the commenting options available in Razor, let's move on and learn about the `<text>` tag.

In some situations you need to write HTML inside code block expressions and wish to display content for better identification, you could do this using the `<text>` tag. Here is an example which will wrap a multi-line content:

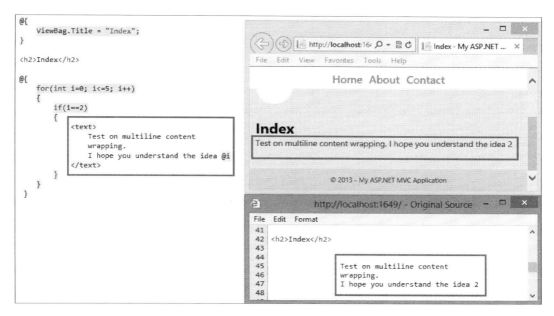

Look at the HTML source code in the preceding screenshot; it does not include any wrapping tags. Optionally, we can wrap the content with a tag such as `<span>`, but this will display the `<span>` tag in the HTML source code as shown in the following screenshot:

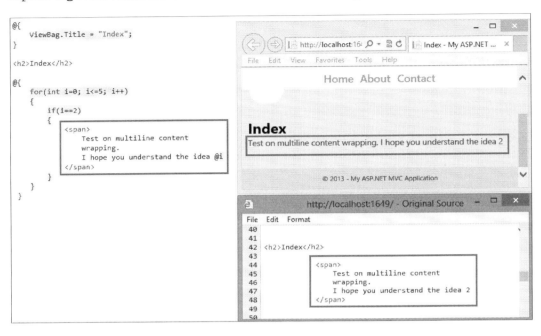

We also have a Razor language parser that enables us to do some heavy lifting. For example, to display the e-mail ID and Twitter handler on a web page, the Razor language parser works cleverly in most cases to infer whether a @ character within a template is used for the code or static content. Take a look at the following example:

```
@{
    ViewBag.Title = "Index";
}

<h2>Index</h2>

You can either tweet me on @itorian or mail me on itorian@live.in
                            The name 'itorian' does not exist in the current context
```

For my e-mail ID, the @ character works cleverly, but for my Twitter handler it didn't. In this case, I can explicitly escape out the @ characters by typing @@; the following screenshot shows you how:

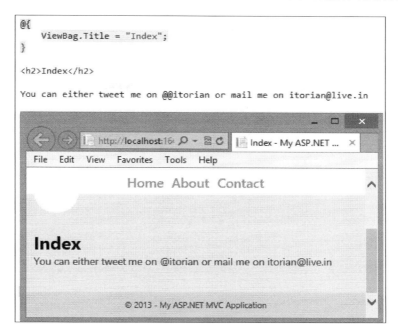

Here is another parsing. You should know here that I am trying to divide the total, which is an integer variable containing 500, by 5, but it is actually concatenating the string instead of dividing.

To overcome this issue, I need to make it an explicit code expression by putting code inside parentheses like (total/5).

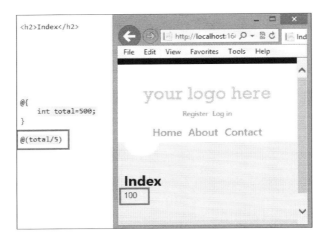

And now we see that it works fine.

That's all you need to know about the fundamental Razor syntaxes. Now you are all set to dig deeper into the Razor view engine.

Razor layout pages (Become an expert)

In this recipe I will introduce you to Razor layout pages, and then we can move forward to cover every single Razor syntax existing in a layout page.

In a web application, it is very important to have content that is displayed on every web page. It may be a header, footer, menus, and so on. It saves a lot of work and centralizes the markup, style, and code which are easier to maintain.

In ASP.NET 2.0, the **master page** concept was introduced to help bring a content block from another file on a web page to **DRY** (**Don't Repeat Yourself**) and to give the web application a consistent look.

In ASP.NET MVC, Razor supports the concept of a **layout page**, which is similar to a master page. A layout page allows us to define a common website template. Let's learn more about the layout page.

Getting ready

In the *Creating the project (Should know)* recipe, we created a project using the **Internet Application** template and the Razor view engine. Open that project and read on reading further.

How to do it...

Before learning Razor layout pages, you should be aware of the _ViewStart.cshtml page. So, first we will look at the _ViewStart.cshtml page and then we will look at the layout page.

1. With the release of ASP.NET MVC 3 Beta, we can now add a file called _ViewStart. cshtml (if the programming language is C#) or _ViewStart.vbhtml (if the programming language is VB) underneath the \Views folder of the ASP.NET MVC projects, which contains the information about the layout page.

2. This _ViewStart.cshtml file can be used to define a common view code that you need to execute at the start of each view; we no longer need to explicitly set the layout in any of our individual view files except if we wanted to override the default value. If you open this file, you will see the following code snippet:

```
@{
    Layout = "~/Views/Shared/_Layout.cshtml";
}
```

3. I could write `Layout = "~/Views/Shared/_Layout.cshtml";` on each view page in the project, but it is not DRY.

```
Index.cshtml  ⊟ ✕  _ViewStart.cshtml
    @{
        ViewBag.Title = "Index";
        Layout = "~/Views/Shared/_Layout.cshtml";
    }

    <h2>Index</h2>
```

4. What DRY does here is it writes `Layout = "~/Views/Shared/_Layout.cshtml";` in the `_ViewStart.cshtml` file. Now, open the `_ViewStart.cshtml` file; the layout filename which is `_Layout.cshtml` by default could be anything else.

```
_ViewStart.cshtml  ⊟ ✕
    @{
        Layout = "~/Views/Shared/_Layout.cshtml";
    }
```

5. We could write the code within the `_ViewStart.cshtml` file to programmatically set the `Layout` property for all views. Depending on the type of device that is accessing the site we can have a phone or tablet to optimize the layout for those devices, and a desktop to optimize the layout for PCs/laptops.

6. Also, what if one wants to apply a new layout to all view pages inside the `Demo` folder? To do this, we could put a `_ViewStart.cshtml` file inside the `/Views/Demo` folder, which would override the default one in the `/Views` folder and specify the desired layout as shown in the following screenshot:

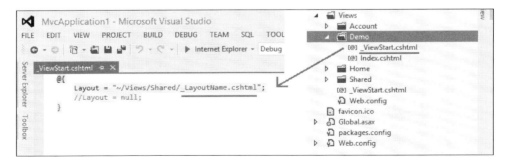

7. If we write `Layout = null;` in the preceding code, it will stop applying any layout to all view pages inside the `\Views\Demo` folder and you will see a layout-free web page. In the case where you don't want any layout, this will work for you.

8. When returning the view inside the controller, we could also specify which layout should be used, the following is an example:

```
return View("Index", "~/Views/Shared/_LayoutName.cshtml",
someViewModel);
```

That's all we need to cover about the `_ViewStart.cshtml` page.

Moving ahead, open the `_Layout.cshtml` file, which can be found in the `/Views/Shared` folder, and have a look at the code; it is shown in the following screenshot:

```
_Layout.cshtml  ⊣ X
    <!DOCTYPE html>
    <html lang="en">
        <head>
            <meta charset="utf-8" />
            <title>@ViewBag.Title - My ASP.NET MVC Application</title>
            <link href="~/favicon.ico" rel="shortcut icon" type="image/x-icon" />
            <meta name="viewport" content="width=device-width" />
            @Styles.Render("~/Content/css")
            @Scripts.Render("~/bundles/modernizr")
        </head>
        <body>
            <header>
                <div class="content-wrapper">
                    <div class="float-left">
                        <p class="site-title">@Html.ActionLink("your logo here", "Index", "Home")</p>
                    </div>
                    <div class="float-right">
                        <section id="login">
                            @Html.Partial("_LoginPartial")
                        </section>
                        <nav>
                            <ul id="menu">
                                <li>@Html.ActionLink("Home", "Index", "Home")</li>
                                <li>@Html.ActionLink("About", "About", "Home")</li>
                                <li>@Html.ActionLink("Contact", "Contact", "Home")</li>
                            </ul>
                        </nav>
                    </div>
                </div>
            </header>
            <div id="body">
                @RenderSection("featured", required: false)
                <section class="content-wrapper main-content clear-fix">
                    @RenderBody()
                </section>
            </div>
            <footer>
                <div class="content-wrapper">
                    <div class="float-left">
                        <p>&copy; @DateTime.Now.Year - My ASP.NET MVC Application</p>
                    </div>
                </div>
            </footer>

            @Scripts.Render("~/bundles/jquery")
            @RenderSection("scripts", required: false)
        </body>
    </html>
```

If you recall, I created this project using the **Internet Application** template in the *Creating the project (Should know)* recipe. This is why we have a ready-to-use layout which has `<head>` and `<body>` sections. In the `<head>` section, we have the title, links, meta, styles, and scripts, and in the `<body>` section we have the site title, menu, login, and so on, which makes a common layout that we can be used to maintain a consistent look and feel across any number of pages on our site.

Don't get confused with the amount of code in the preceding screenshot, they are pretty simple to understand. I'll discuss what each piece of code means, one by one, in a bit. Some of them will be discussed in the next recipe.

`RenderBody()`, which is a Razor syntax, is equivalent to `ContentPlaceHolder`, which is an ASPX syntax. In this code, we are calling the `RenderBody()` method within the layout file to indicate where we want the views based on this layout to "fill in" their core content at that location in the HTML. The following screenshot gives us an explanation:

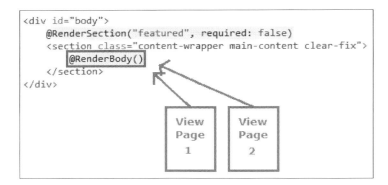

Here, **View Page 1** is just like the `About.cshtml` view page, and **View Page 2** is like the `Contact.cshtml` view page, and so on. In the `About.cshtml` or `Contact.cshtml` view page, we do not need to wrap our main body content within a tag or element; by default Razor will automatically treat the content as the body section of the layout page. We can optionally define named sections if our layout has multiple replaceable regions; you will learn it in this recipe.

`ViewBag.Title` is used to output the `View.Title` property within the `<title>` element of our `<head>` section, shown in the following screenshot:

```
<head>
    <meta charset="utf-8" />
    <title>@ViewBag.Title - My ASP.NET MVC Application</title>
    <link href="~/favicon.ico" rel="shortcut icon" type="image/x-icon" />
    <meta name="viewport" content="width=device-width" />
    @Styles.Render("~/Content/css")
    @Scripts.Render("~/bundles/modernizr")
</head>
```

To understand this, open any view page; you will notice the `ViewBag.Title` property is assigned with a value, in this case we have `Index`, and now our `<title>` will become `Index - My ASP.NET MVC Application`:

```
Index.cshtml  ⊣  X
    @{
        ViewBag.Title = "Index";
    }

    <h2>Index</h2>
```

`ViewBag` is a very well-known way to pass the data from controller to view and even from view to view. `ViewBag` uses the dynamic feature that was added in C# 4.0. In the preceding screenshot, we are programmatically setting the `ViewBag.Title` value within our `Index.cshtml` page. The code within our `Index.cshtml` file will run before the `_Layout.cshtml` code runs and so we can write the view code that programmatically sets values we want to pass to our layout to render. This is particularly useful for things such as setting the page's title, as well as `<meta>` elements within the `<head>` for SEO.

The `System.Web.Optimization` namespace has two awesome helpers, `@Styles.Render` and `@Scripts.Render`, which help us to perform **Bundling and Minification**. Minimizing the number of requests the page has to perform can have a considerable effect on our site's performance. Bundling and Minification are very common scenarios that help to reduce the number of requests and file size by bundling (that is, all CSS and JS files into two separate files) and minifying (that is, removing blank spaces that are not required, removing comments, and reducing identifiers).

Bundling and Minification is performed at runtime, so that the process can identify the user agent (for example IE, Mozilla, and so on), and thus improve the compression by targeting the user browser (for instance, removing stuff that is Mozilla-specific when the request comes from IE).

```
<head>
    <meta charset="utf-8" />
    <title>@ViewBag.Title - My ASP.NET MVC Application</title>
    <link href="~/favicon.ico" rel="shortcut icon" type="image/x-icon" />
    <meta name="viewport" content="width=device-width" />
    @Styles.Render("~/Content/css")
    @Scripts.Render("~/bundles/modernizr")
</head>
```

The code in the preceding screenshot actually calls the files included in that particular bundle, which is declared inside the `BundleConfig` class in the `App_Start` folder. Open this file, it should be as follows:

```
BundleConfig.cs   + X
MvcApplication1.BundleConfig                                                               RegisterBun

using System.Web;
using System.Web.Optimization;

namespace MvcApplication1
{
    public class BundleConfig
    {
        // For more information on Bundling, visit http://go.microsoft.com/fwlink/?LinkId=254725
        public static void RegisterBundles(BundleCollection bundles)
        {
            bundles.Add(new ScriptBundle("~/bundles/jquery").Include(
                        "~/Scripts/jquery-{version}.js"));

            bundles.Add(new ScriptBundle("~/bundles/jqueryui").Include(
                        "~/Scripts/jquery-ui-{version}.js"));

            bundles.Add(new ScriptBundle("~/bundles/jqueryval").Include(
                        "~/Scripts/jquery.unobtrusive*",
                        "~/Scripts/jquery.validate*"));

            // Use the development version of Modernizr to develop with and learn from. Then, when you're
            // ready for production, use the build tool at http://modernizr.com to pick only the tests you need.
            bundles.Add(new ScriptBundle("~/bundles/modernizr").Include(
                        "~/Scripts/modernizr-*"));

            bundles.Add(new StyleBundle("~/Content/css").Include("~/Content/site.css"));

            bundles.Add(new StyleBundle("~/Content/themes/base/css").Include(
                        "~/Content/themes/base/jquery.ui.core.css",
                        "~/Content/themes/base/jquery.ui.resizable.css",
                        "~/Content/themes/base/jquery.ui.selectable.css",
                        "~/Content/themes/base/jquery.ui.accordion.css",
                        "~/Content/themes/base/jquery.ui.autocomplete.css",
                        "~/Content/themes/base/jquery.ui.button.css",
                        "~/Content/themes/base/jquery.ui.dialog.css",
                        "~/Content/themes/base/jquery.ui.slider.css",
                        "~/Content/themes/base/jquery.ui.tabs.css",
                        "~/Content/themes/base/jquery.ui.datepicker.css",
                        "~/Content/themes/base/jquery.ui.progressbar.css",
                        "~/Content/themes/base/jquery.ui.theme.css"));
        }
    }
}
```

In that particular case the call to `@Styles.Render("~/Content/css")` is made to call `"~/Content/site.css"`.

As we know, layouts in Razor serve the same purpose as master pages do in Web Forms. They allow you to specify a layout for your site and create a placeholder for your views to implement. Open the `_Layout.cshtml` file, you will see a section called `featured`, which is an optional section just above `@RenderBody()`, highlighted in the following screenshot:

```
<div id="body">
    @RenderSection("featured", required: false)
    <section class="content-wrapper main-content clear-fix">
        @RenderBody()
    </section>
</div>
```

Now, on any view page, if I want a `featured` section to appear, I could write following:

Using Razor, we can also check the existence of a section on a view page (`Index.cshtml`) from the layout (`_Layout.cshtml`) page, and depending upon its existence, we can display the alternative information.

In the following example, using the `IsSectionDefined()` method, we can check if the section has been defined on the view page or not. If it is not defined, the alternative information will be rendered.

```
<div id="body">
    @if (IsSectionDefined("featured")) {
        @RenderSection("featured", required: false)
    }
    else {
        <p>
            Alternative Information
        </p>
    }
    <section class="content-wrapper main-content clear-fix">
        @RenderBody()
    </section>
</div>
```

On the `Index.cshtml` view page, I would not like the `featured` section to appear, so I'll not write it and Razor will display **Alternative Information**, as shown in the following screenshot:

Razor layout pages are equivalent to master pages in ASP.NET Web Forms. Just as it is possible to nest master pages, it is also possible to nest Razor layout pages.

To tryout an example of a nested layout page, create a new project with the **Empty Project** template. Please don't mix it in the project that we already have in place.

Consider a web application that has header and footer sections. The footer section will be visible to all but I would the like header section to be invisible to the admins. I would like to define a nested layout to enable this feature.

1. Create a file in `Views/Shared/_Layout.cshtml` and write the following code in it. This is a top-level layout but looks like a regular Razor layout.

```
<!DOCTYPE html>
<html lang="en">
    <head>
        <title>@ViewBag.Title</title>
    </head>
    <body>
        @RenderSection("header", required: false)
        @RenderBody()
        @RenderSection("footer", required: false)
    </body>
</html>
```

2. Now, let's create a public-specific layout file in `Views/Shared/_PublicLayout.cshtml` and write the following code:

```
@{
    Layout = "~/Views/Shared/_Layout.cshtml";
}

<p>Hello from Public layout.</p>

@section header{
    <p>
        header information goes here.
    </p>
}

@RenderBody()

@section footer{
    <p>
        footer information goes here.
    </p>
}
```

In this code, first I defined which layout page this layout will inherit, and then I defined both the header and footer sections, including a `RenderBody()` call.

3. Now, let's create an admin-specific layout file in `Views/Shared/_AdminLayout.cshtml` and write the following code:

```
@{
    Layout = "~/Views/Shared/_Layout.cshtml";
}

<p>Hello from Admin layout.</p>

@RenderBody()

@section footer{
    <p>
        footer information goes here.
    </p>
}
```

In this code, first I defined which layout page this layout will inherit and then I defined only the footer section and a `RenderBody()` call.

We are all set to test nested layouts. To test the public layout, add a view as given in the following screenshot and look at the output. Remember to point to the `_PublicLayout.cshtml` layout when adding any public view.

To test the admin layout, add a view as given in the following screenshot and look at the output:

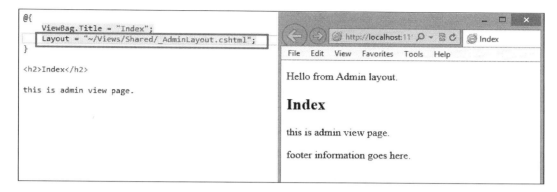

You must have noticed that we can't see the **header information goes here** message in the admin layout. I hope you get the idea of using nested layouts.

How it works...

Razor is flexible enough so that we can make changes like the ones we saw in this recipe, without having to modify any of our view templates (nor make any controller logic changes) to accommodate this. We can instead make minimal modifications to our layout file and the rest happens cleanly. This type of flexibility makes Razor incredibly powerful and productive.

There's more...

The design (look and feel) of the ASP.NET MVC application is completely dependent on the _Layout.cshtml and Site.css files. So, to get a new look and feel, you have to update these files.

Models in Razor (Must know)

In this recipe, I will introduce you to the Razor model directive by comparing it with the @inherits directive, and then we'll set up a model class to show you how to scaffold views and also how to add views manually.

Getting ready

The @model directive announced with the release of ASP.NET MVC 3 Beta provides a cleaner and more concise way to reference strongly-typed models from view files than the @inherits directive, which was announced with the first ASP.NET MVC 3 preview.

In MVC, we can have strongly-typed views or loosely-coupled views, the main difference between the two being that strongly-typed views give us the benefit of IntelliSense; on the other hand, IntelliSense is not available with loosely-typed views.

To learn more about @inherits and @model directives, let's create a new data model class and scaffold the CRUD views using Code First Approach in Entity Framework. The goal of this model will be to allow the user to create and manage a To-Do list.

- ▶ **Entity Framework (EF)** is an **Object-Relational Mapper (ORM)** that enables .NET developers to work with relational data using domain-specific objects. It is an enhancement to ADO.NET that gives developers an automated mechanism for accessing and storing the data in the database and working with the results in addition to DataReader and DataSet.

- ▶ **Code First Approach** provides an alternative to the Database First and Model First approaches to the Entity data model and creates a database for us. This enables a pretty sweet development workflow and lets you define model objects by simply writing classes.

How to do it...

Model manages the behavior and data in the application and responds to requests for information. So, let's create a sample model to manage a To-Do list.

Creating a data model class

Right-click on the model folder and add a class file called ToDo.cs and add the following code:

```
ToDo.cs  ⊕  ×
❖$ MvcApplication1.Models.ToDo
⊟using System;
  using System.Collections.Generic;
  using System.ComponentModel;
  using System.ComponentModel.DataAnnotations;
  using System.Linq;
  using System.Web;

⊟namespace MvcApplication1.Models
  {
⊟     public class ToDo
      {
          public int ToDoId { get; set; }

          [Required]
          public string Title { get; set; }

          [Required]
          [DataType(DataType.MultilineText)]
          public string Description { get; set; }

          [DisplayName("Is Done")]
          public bool IsDone { get; set; }
      }
  }
```

In this code, I have added four properties: `ToDoId`, `Title`, `Description`, and `IsDone`. I have added the `[Required]` attribute with the property `Title` and `Description`, which specifies that a data field is required. I have also added `[DataType(DataType.MultilineText)]` which specifies that the data field is multiline. So, these are declarative validation attribute rules which will automatically be enforced whenever ASP.NET MVC performs model binding operations within an application. Remember to add a namespace, `System.ComponentModel.DataAnnotations`, at the top of the file. In addition with the validation attribute I have also used a `[DisplayName("Is Done")]` attribute with the `IsDone` property, and this will display "Is Done" instead of "IsDone" on the view. This attribute is derived from the `System.ComponentModel` namespace.

Data annotations help us to define the rules with semantic attributes such as `[Required]`, `[DataType]`, and `[DisplayName]` to the model classes or properties for data validation and displaying suitable messages to the end users.

Scaffolding view templates

Scaffolding is a technique used in MVC to quickly generate views, controllers, databases, table scripts, and so on, and allows us to **Create, Read, Update**, and **Delete** records (also known as **CRUD**) with the help of Entity Framework.

When you are done with the model, build the solution from the **Build** menu. Now, right-click on the `controller` folder to add a new controller. The following dialog box will appear:

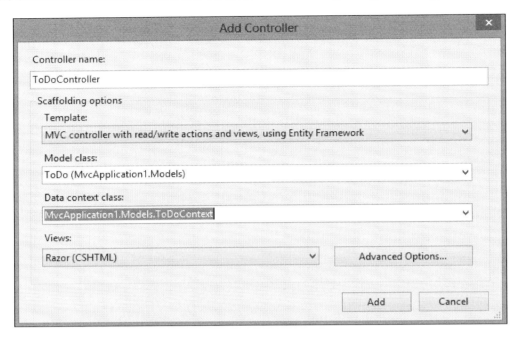

In the **Add Controller** dialog box, use the controller name to `ToDoController`. I am going to scaffold the CRUD views using Entity Framework, so select the appropriate template and model class as shown in the preceding screenshot. Also, we don't have any data context as of now, so add a new one from the drop-down list. At the end, click on the **Add** button and this will add all the CRUD views and controllers on the fly.

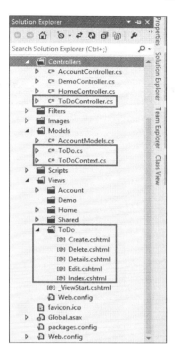

Run the application and navigate to the **ToDo** controller and try creating a blank entry; you will see the validations in action.

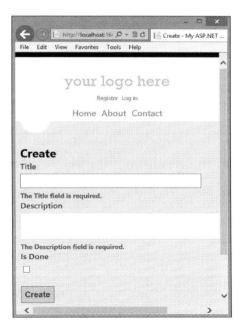

Now, create your To-Do list. In the following screenshot, you can see that I have added four To-do items. You will notice that the title name for the IsDone column is **Is Done** (with space), this is because of the [DisplayName("Is Done")] attribute that we have added with the model property.

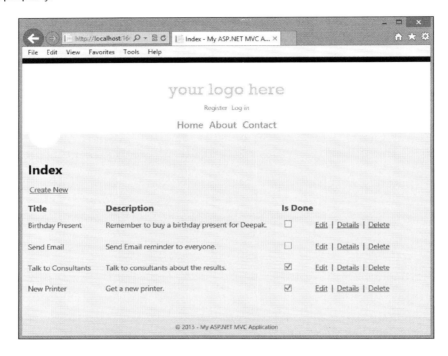

Now, we are all set to learn the @inherits and @model directives.

@inherits and @model directives

Open the Index.cshtml file from the Views/ToDo folder and look at the first line of code, highlighted in the following screenshot:

```
ToDoController.cs    Index.cshtml  ⊣ ✕  Details.cshtml    Create.

    @model IEnumerable<MvcApplication1.Models.ToDo>

    @{
        ViewBag.Title = "Index";
    }

    <h2>Index</h2>

    <p>
        @Html.ActionLink("Create New", "Create")
    </p>
    <table>
```

The code line `@model IEnumerable<MvcApplication1.Models.ToDo>` is very similar to `@inherits System.Web.Mvc.WebViewPage<IEnumerable<MvcApplication1.Models.ToDo>>`. So, using `@inherits System.Web.Mvc.WebViewPage<IEnumerable<MvcApplication1.Models.ToDo>>` at the top of the file works fine but it is a little verbose. So, it is more common to use `@model IEnumerable<MvcApplication1.Models.ToDo>` at the top of the file and then you don't need to have `@inherits` or specify a view base class anymore; this is power of Razor.

Now, once you have the model on the view, we can do anything. For instance, to display the first To-Do item I could write the following code:

```
Index.cshtml  ⊕ ✕   ToDoController.cs
    @model IEnumerable<MvcApplication1.Models.ToDo>

    @{
        ViewBag.Title = "Index";
    }

    <h2>Index</h2>

    @{
        var first = Model.First();
    }

    <b>@first.Title</b>
    @first.Description
```

It will also display the first To-Do `Title` and `Description`.

This is all about the new `@model` directive. We have scaffolded all the required view templates till now, however, we can manually add the different views one by one, but before doing this I will recommend you to delete the `ToDo View` folder with all its views to avoid delicacy. Let's learn them now.

Manually adding view templates

First, to display the list of To-Do items we need a controller action that we already have. Open `ToDoController` from the `Controller` folder, and you will see the following code:

```
public class ToDoController : Controller
{
    private ToDoContext db = new ToDoContext();

    //
    // GET: /ToDo/

    public ActionResult Index()
    {
        return View(db.ToDoes.ToList());
    }
}
```

In the first highlighted rectangular region, we have an instance of the database context, and in the second region we have an action method called `Index` which will return the list of To-Do items. Now, to add the view for this `Index` action method, we need to right-click inside this method and select **Add View...**, as shown in the following screenshot:

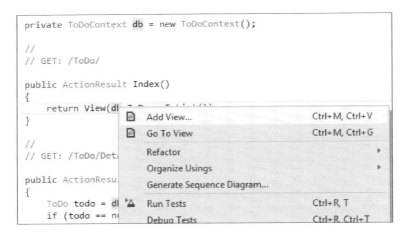

When you click on **Add View...**, you will see the following dialog box:

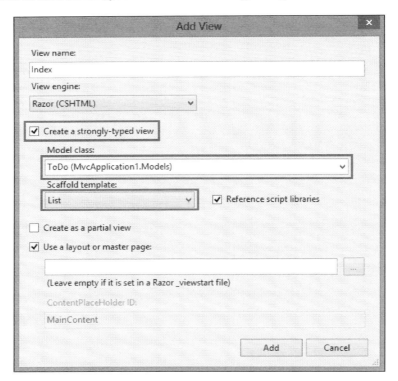

In the **Add View** dialog box, remember to check the **Create a strongly-typed view** checkbox, select the **ToDo** model class, and set the **Scaffold template** option to **List**. When you are done, click on the **Add** button. This will create exactly the same `Index.cshtml` view page that the earlier scaffold does. In the same way, we can scaffold views for `Details`, `Create`, `Edit`, and `Delete` action methods.

If you open the `Index.cshtml` view page, you will see the following code:

```
@foreach (var item in Model) {
    <tr>
        <td>
            @Html.DisplayFor(modelItem => item.Title)
        </td>
        <td>
            @Html.DisplayFor(modelItem => item.Description)
        </td>
        <td>
            @Html.DisplayFor(modelItem => item.IsDone)
        </td>
        <td>
            @Html.ActionLink("Edit", "Edit", new { id=item.ToDoId }) |
            @Html.ActionLink("Details", "Details", new { id=item.ToDoId }) |
            @Html.ActionLink("Delete", "Delete", new { id=item.ToDoId })
        </td>
    </tr>
```

In this code, for each `modelItem` I'm creating one `<tr>` and four `<td>` tags that will display `Title`, `Description`, `IsDone`, and `Edit/Details/Delete` links.

There's more...

If you open the CRUD views that we created earlier, you will see many HTML helpers that are being used, and in the next recipe we will look at helpers used in Razor.

Razor helpers (Must know)

In this recipe, you will learn how to create helpers with the extension method as well as with the declarative `@helper` syntax. In addition to this, we will see a list of the most frequently used standard helpers such as input helpers, link helpers, form helpers, label helpers, and validation message helpers.

Getting ready

The previous versions of MVC introduced an extension method of the `HtmlHelper` class that allowed you to define new helpers. In MVC 3 you have an option to continue doing that, however you can also use a declarative helper using the `@helper` syntax within a Razor view. So, first you will look at the extension method approach and then we will look at the `@helper` syntax approach, and at the end we will also look at the other standard helpers.

How to do it...

This recipe is going to focuses completely on helpers so let's begin by creating a helper with the extension method.

HTML helpers using the extension method

The new HTML helpers created by the extension method of the `HtmlHelper` class work just like the standard HTML helpers (at the end of this recipe you will learn about standard HTML helpers). Let's recall, in the last recipe we created a To-Do list, shown in the following screenshot:

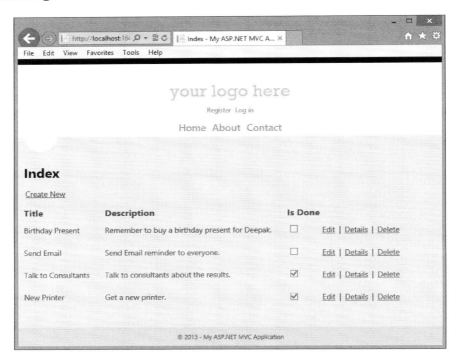

I need to safeguard myself when the **Description** area gets very long, which can break the look of my page. Thus, I need to truncate the description message by setting the maximum length, say, to 40 characters to be displayed, and when the maximum length is crossed it should display **...more** at the end. To see more of the description, the user should click on the **Details** link. The following screenshot shows the output screen:

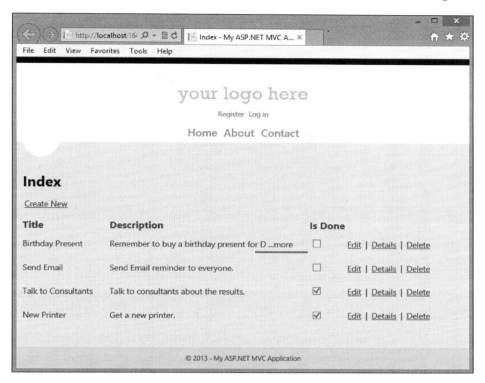

In the preceding screenshot you can see the **...more** character is truncated at the end of the first To-Do item description. This can be done using the extension methods. Let's develop this by adding a new class named `HtmlHelpers.cs`.

```
HtmlHelpers.cs
MvcApplication1.Helpers.HtmlHelpers                                    Truncate(HtmlHelper helper,
using System;
using System.Collections.Generic;
using System.Linq;
using System.Web;
using System.Web.Mvc;

namespace MvcApplication1.Helpers
{
    public static class HtmlHelpers
    {
        public static string Truncate(this HtmlHelper helper, string input, int length)
        {
            if (input.Length <= length)
                return input;
            else
                return input.Substring(0, length) + " ...more";
        }
    }
}
```

In the preceding screenshot, we added an extension method to the `HtmlHelper` class named `Truncate()`. There are a couple of things that you should notice about this class. First, notice that the class is a static class. You must define an extension method with a static class. Second, notice that the first parameter of the `Truncate()` method is preceded by the keyword `this`. The first parameter of an extension method, which is `this HtmlHelper helper`, indicates the class that the extension method extends to and it is derived from the namespace `System.Web.Mvc`. This `Truncate()` method will accept two parameters, the input string and length. In the method body, We need to check if the length of the input string is less than or equal to the length. If it is then keep it as it is, or else return the substring of the input string by concatenating **...more** in the string. Let's see how the view page will utilize this extension method:

```
Index.cshtml  ₽ ×  HtmlHelpers.cs
    @model IEnumerable<MvcApplication1.Models.ToDo>

    @using MvcApplication1.Helpers

    @{
        ViewBag.Title = "Index";
    }

    <h2>Index</h2>

    <p>...</p>
    <table>
        <tr>...</tr>

    @foreach (var item in Model) {
        <tr>
            <td>
                @Html.DisplayFor(modelItem => item.Title)
            </td>
            <td>
                @*@Html.DisplayFor(modelItem => item.Description)*@
                @Html.Truncate(item.Description, 40)
            </td>
            <td>
                @Html.DisplayFor(modelItem => item.IsDone)
            </td>
```

To bring the scope of the newly-added extension methods on a view page we have added the `MvcApplication1.Helpers` namespace; alternatively, we can also add this namespace directly into `web.config` to use it in a whole application. Now, instead of using `@Html. DisplayFor()`, I would use my extension method `@Html.Truncate()` and pass two parameters `item.Description`, which is string and `40`, which is a `int` value and I'm done.

Now, what if I want to display ...more in red color? The extension method returns a string value so we can embed the HTML markups in that string.

```
public static string Truncate(this HtmlHelper helper, string input, int length)
{
    if (input.Length <= length)
        return input;
    else
        //return input.Substring(0, length) + " ...more";
        return input.Substring(0, length) + "<span style=\"color:red;\"> ...more<span>";
}
```

In Razor, the @ character is HTML encoded by default for better protection against XSS attacks. Thus, on the view page we will use the @Html.Row() helper:

```
<td>
    @*@Html.DisplayFor(modelItem => item.Description)*@
    @Html.Raw(@Html.Truncate(item.Description, 40))
</td>
```

Now, you will have the desired output on your screen.

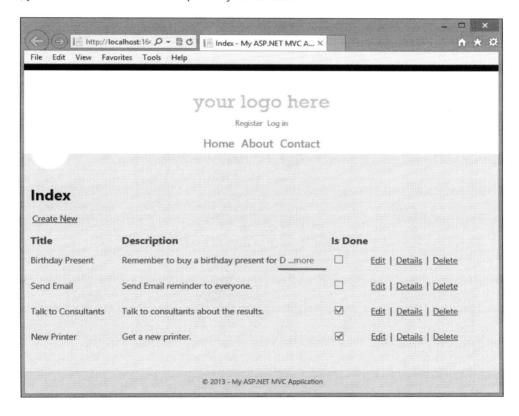

All this can be done by simply using declarative @helper syntax, let's learn it.

HTML helpers using the @helper syntax

In Razor, we can declare the @helper syntax on the same view page or create it in a separate file. First we will see how to declare it on the same view page.

```
Index.cshtml    X  HtmlHelpers.cs
    @model IEnumerable<MvcApplication1.Models.ToDo>

    @{
        ViewBag.Title = "Index";
    }

    @helper Truncate(string input, int length)
    {
        if(input.Length <= length) {
            @input
        } else {
            @input.Substring(0, length)<text> ...more</text>
        }
    }

    <h2>Index</h2>

    <p>...</p>
    <table>
        <tr>...</tr>

    @foreach (var item in Model) {
        <tr>
            <td>
                @Html.DisplayFor(modelItem => item.Title)
            </td>
            <td>
                @Truncate(item.Description, 40)
            </td>
            <td>
                @Html.DisplayFor(modelItem => item.IsDone)
            </td>
```

In the previous screenshot, I declared @helper by the name Truncate, which will accept only two parameters, the input string and length. To call this @helper Truncate(), you just have to use @Truncate(item.Description, 40). That's all.

Now, if you want to move @helper Truncate() into a separate file, we can do this by adding a new .cshtml view page file inside the App_Code folder and paste all the @helper Truncate() code, and at the end call @helper Truncate() using @HtmlHelpers.Truncate(item.Description, 40).

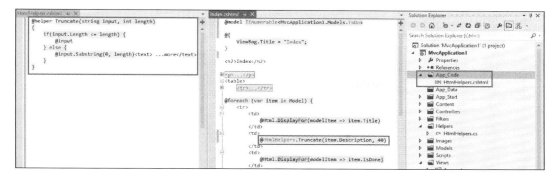

If you run this application, you will have the same output.

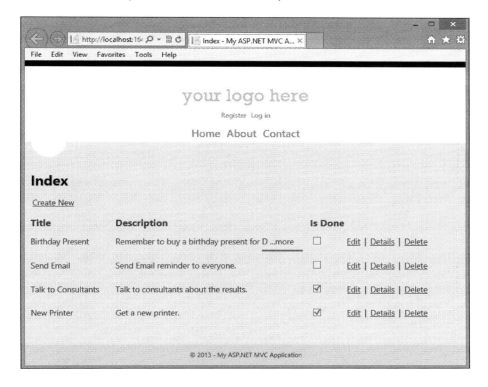

So far in this recipe you learned how to create HTML helpers with the extension method and with declarative @helper syntax. Now, let's learn about some standard HTML helpers.

Standard HTML helpers

The HTML helpers that we have seen so far in this recipe return a string, and that string can represent any type of content that you want on the view page. The main purpose of any HTML helper is to create small blocks of HTML, and that can be categorized into input helpers, link helpers, form helpers, validation messages helpers, label helpers, and more.

Input helpers

Razor includes a set of standard HTML input helpers; I have listed some of them in the following table:

HTML helper	HTML element	Short description
`@Html.CheckBox(s:name, b:checked)`	`<input type="checkbox" name="name" id="name" checked="checked" />`	Returns a checkbox input element.
`@Html.CheckBoxFor(e:expression)`	`<input type="checkbox" name="name" id="name" checked="checked" />`	Returns a checkbox input element for the model.
`@Html.DropDownList(s:name, list:selectlistitems)`	`<select name="name" id="name"></select>`	Returns a single-selection select element.
`@Html.DropDownListFor(e:expression, list:selectlistitems)`	`<select name="name" id="name"></select>`	Returns a single-selection select element for the model.
`@Html.Hidden(s:name, o:value)`	`<input type="hidden" value="value" name="name" />`	Returns a hidden input element.
`@Html.HiddenFor(e:expression)`	`<input type="hidden" value="value" name="name" />`	Returns a hidden input element for the model.
`@Html.ListBox(s:name, list:selectlistitems)`	`<select multiple="multiple" name="name" id="name"></select>`	Returns a multi-select select element.
`@Html.ListBoxFor(e:expression, list:selectlistitems)`	`<select multiple="multiple" name="name" id="name"></select>`	Returns a multi-select select element for the model.

HTML helper	HTML element	Short description
`@Html.Password(s:name, o:value)`	`<input type="password" value="value" name="name" />`	Returns a password input element.
`@Html. PasswordFor(e:expression)`	`<input type="password" value="value" name="name" />`	Returns a password input element for the model.
`@Html.RadioButton(s:name, o:value, b:checked)`	`<input type="radio" value="value" name="name" checked="checked" />`	Returns a radio button input element.
`@Html. RadioButtonFor(e:expression, o:value)`	`<input type="radio" value="value" name="name" checked="checked" />`	Returns a radio button input element for the model.
`@Html.TextArea(s:name, s:value)`	`<textarea name="name">value</ textarea>`	Returns the specified textarea element.
`@Html. TextAreaFor(e:expression)`	`<textarea name="name">value</ textarea>`	Returns the specified textarea element for the model.
`@Html.TextBox(s:name, o:value)`	`<input type="text" name="name" value="value" />`	Returns a text input element.
`@Html. TextBoxFor(e:expression)`	`<input type="text" name="name" value="value" />`	Returns a text input element for the model.

If you look at the list of Input helpers, you will notice that each helper has two versions such as `CheckBox` and `CheckBoxFor`, `TextBox` and `TextBoxFor`, `TextArea` and `TextAreaFor`.

Helpers such as `CheckBox`, `TextBox`, and `TextArea` work fine but they don't allow coding in the strongly-typed fashion and you need to hardcode whatever name you want as the first argument:

```
@Html.TextArea("Description")
```

So, in Razor we have a model version of helpers such as `CheckBoxFor`, `TextBoxFor`, and `TextAreaFor` that require a strongly-typed view and use the view model:

```
@Html.TextAreaFor(model => model.Description)
```

The helpers will use the lambda expression to infer the name and the value of the view model passed to the view. And because it is a good practice to use strongly-typed views and view models, you should always use the `@Html.TextBoxFor` helper.

By default, the `Create` and `Edit` scaffolds now use the `@Html.EditorFor` helper instead of the `@Html.TextBoxFor` helper. The `@Html.EditorFor` helper works by examining the model type passed to it; for instance, if the model type is `Boolean`, `EditorFor` will generate a checkbox; if model type is `text`, `EditorFor` will generate an input box. `EditorFor` also improves the support for metadata on the model in the form of data annotation attributes.

In Razor, sometimes we also use another model version of helpers such as `DisplayForModel()`, `DisplayNameForModel()`, `EditorForModel()`, `NameForModel`, `LabelForModel`, and `ValueForModel` that return HTML markup for every property in the model. Let's look at an example of `DisplayForModel()`:

```
@*<div class="display-label">
        @Html.DisplayNameFor(model => model.Title)
</div>
<div class="display-field">
    @Html.DisplayFor(model => model.Title)
</div>

<div class="display-label">
        @Html.DisplayNameFor(model => model.Description)
</div>
<div class="display-field">
    @Html.DisplayFor(model => model.Description)
</div>*@

@Html.DisplayForModel()
```

In this code, I commented all the `<div>` blocks and instead of writing four `<div>` elements we can achieve the same with the `@Html.DisplayForModel()` helper, and it works great.

Form helpers

Razor also includes a set of standard HTML form helpers; I have listed some of them in the following table:

HTML helper	HTML element	Short description
`@Html.AntiForgeryToken (s:salt, s:domain, s:path)`	`<input type="hidden" value="token" name="name" />`	Generates a hidden `form` field that is validated when the form is submitted.
`@Html.BeginForm (s:action, s:controller, o:values)`	`<form action="/ controller/action/">`	Writes an opening `<form>` tag to the response. The request will be processed by the `action` method.
`@Html.BeginRouteForm (s:routeName)`	`<form action="route">`	Writes an opening `<form>` tag for the route. The request will be processed by the `route` target.
`@Html.EndForm()`	`</form>`	Renders the closing `</ form>` tag to the response.
`@Html.AttributeEncode (s:input)`	-	Converts the specified string to an HTML-encoded string.
`@Html.Encode(o:object)`	-	Converts the specified string to an HTML-encoded string.

The `AntiForgeryToken` helper is used to prevent **Cross Site Request Forgery** (**CSRF**) or XSRF attacks. We put the user-specific token as a `hidden` field on the form, as given in the following code:

```
@using (Html.BeginForm())
{
    @Html.ValidationSummary(true)
    @Html.AntiForgeryToken()
    <fieldset>
        <legend>Profile</legend>
        <div class="editor-label">
            @Html.LabelFor(model => model.Name)
        </div>
```

Then, an attribute is applied to the controller action, which checks the right value submitted with each `Post` request.

```
[HttpPost]
[ValidateAntiForgeryToken]
public ActionResult Edit(Profile profile)
{
    if (ModelState.IsValid)
    {
```

If you view the view source you will notice the following `hidden` input field with a very long token value.

```
<input name="__RequestVerificationToken" type="hidden"
value="cUcTSMC6k4jcDPan1J-qyv--Tcot4Cu8Nma57-NrbkHc6aaV-
TkQeQChgSRWSEplMRtj-bliGHFj6UuwrvpLu6-S8qiWci8yyHusroPuWzciNmLRw5YbyG
sp_orI4F_q5XouPcbD0F_keLfbKXdMnqS1ZHce-pars_kMxN-flEI1" />
```

When the form `Post` occurs, it compares the issued verification token value on the server and ensures that they match.

Validation helpers

Razor also includes a set of standard HTML validation helpers; I have listed some of them in the following table:

Helper	Short description
@Html.Validate	Retrieves the validation metadata for the specified model and applies each rule to the data field.
@Html.ValidateFor()	Retrieves the validation metadata for the specified model and applies each rule to the data field.
@Html.ValidationMessage()	Displays a validation message if an error exists for the specified field in the `System.Web.Mvc.ModelState.Dictionary` object.
@Html.ValidationMessageFor()	Returns the HTML markup for a validation-error message for each data field that is represented by the specified expression, using the specified message and HTML attributes.
@Html.ValidationSummery()	Returns an unordered list of validation messages that are in the `System.Web.Mvc.ModelStateDictionary` object and optionally displays only model-level errors.

Link helpers

Razor also includes a set of standard HTML link helpers; I have listed some of them in the following table:

HTML helper	HTML element	Short description
@Html.ActionLink (s:text, s:action)	`<a href="action"> text</a>`	Creates an anchor tag to a link for a specific action.
@Html. RouteLink(s:text, s:routeName)	–	Returns an anchor element that contains the virtual path of the specified action.

HTML helper	HTML element	Short description
@Html. RouteLink(s:text, s:routeName)	–	Returns an anchor element that contains the virtual path of the specified action.
@Html. Action(s:action, s:controller)	–	Returns the result as an HTML string.
@Html. Partial(s:name, o:model)	–	Returns the result as an HTML string.

Label helpers

Razor also includes a set of standard HTML label helpers; I have listed some of them in the following table:

Helper	HTML element	Short description
@Html.Label(s:text)	<label for="control"> text</label>	Returns an HTML label element and the property name of the property that is represented by the specified expression.
@Html. LabelFor(e:expression)	<label for="control"> text</label>	Returns an HTML label element and the property name of the property that is represented by the specified expression.
@Html.LabelForModel()	<label for="control"> text</label>	Returns an HTML label element and the property name of the property that is represented by the specified expression using the label text.

How it works...

Most of the Razor helpers we learned in this section generate HTML elements on the form, we saw some helpers that do not generate HTML element, rather they bring the HTML content from other partial views. In the next recipe, we will look at the partial views.

There's more...

We learned enough about Razor helpers in this recipe, however, there are a few more helpers. You can find them at http://goo.gl/0v4DQ.

Partial views (Should know)

In this recipe, we will look at what a partial view is and then we will learn how to render partial views using `Partial`, `RenderPartial`, `Action`, and `RenderAction` helper methods. I will also show you how to render them using jQuery.

Getting ready

Partial views allow us to put HTML and C# code into a file that we can reuse across multiple other views. It is like a user control in ASP.NET Web Forms that also allows the reusing of code. With the help of partial views we can reduce the duplication of code.

How to do it...

Let's quickly start by learning `Partial` and `RenderPartial` and later we will talk about `Action` and RenderAction helper methods.

The main difference between `Partial` and `RenderPartial` is that `Partial` returns an `MvcHtmlString`, whereas `RenderPartial` returns void and renders directly to the view, and because of this, `RenderPartial` works a bit faster.

Partial helper

This helper is used to render the specified partial view as an HTML-encoded string. Also, it is very easy to use and does not need to create any action.

To explore this, go to the *Models in Razor (Should know)* recipe in which we created CRUD views, and open the `Index.cshtml` file.

```
@foreach (var item in Model) {
    <tr>
        <td>
            @Html.DisplayFor(modelItem => item.Title)
        </td>
        <td>
            @Html.DisplayFor(modelItem => item.Description)
        </td>
        <td>
            @Html.DisplayFor(modelItem => item.IsDone)
        </td>
        <td>
            @Html.ActionLink("Edit", "Edit", new { id=item.ToDoId }) |
            @Html.ActionLink("Details", "Details", new { id=item.ToDoId }) |
            @Html.ActionLink("Delete", "Delete", new { id=item.ToDoId })
        </td>
    </tr>
}
</table>
```

In this code, you can see that I am looping through each record in the model using the foreach loop. This produces the following output:

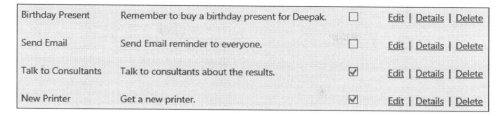

Birthday Present	Remember to buy a birthday present for Deepak.	☐	Edit | Details | Delete
Send Email	Send Email reminder to everyone.	☐	Edit | Details | Delete
Talk to Consultants	Talk to consultants about the results.	☑	Edit | Details | Delete
New Printer	Get a new printer.	☑	Edit | Details | Delete

In case we need this view somewhere else in the website, the best way to do this is by creating a partial view with the code we selected earlier and then render it in the view using a set of helpers.

To do this, follow these steps:

1. Right-click on the folder to add a partial view. You can add it inside the controller's own `View` folder or inside the `Shared` folder for application-level availability.

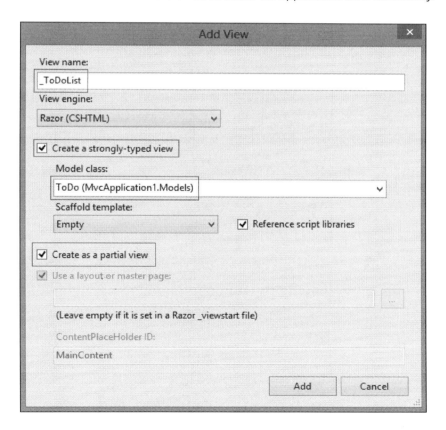

It is a best practice to name the partial view preceded by an underscore character (_), but it is not mandatory. The underscore character (_) before the view name specifies that it is a reusable component. You can create a strongly-typed view by checking it and selecting the `Model` class name, however, that is also not mandatory, as you can go with a simple name. Don't forget to check **Create as a partial view**.

2. Now, in the opened partial view page add the following code. This code snippet is very similar to earlier one that I selected in the rectangle in the first screenshot of this section.

```
@model MvcApplication1.Models.ToDo

<tr>
    <td>
        @Html.DisplayFor(model => model.Title)
    </td>
    <td>
        @Html.DisplayFor(model => model.Description)
    </td>
    <td>
        @Html.DisplayFor(model => model.IsDone)
    </td>
    <td>
        @Html.ActionLink("Edit", "Edit", new { id=Model.ToDoId })
|
        @Html.ActionLink("Details", "Details", new { id=Model.
ToDoId }) |
        @Html.ActionLink("Delete", "Delete", new { id=Model.ToDoId
})
    </td>
</tr>
```

In this code, I have made some quick modifications to match the model convention. Now this partial view is ready to be used anywhere in the application, by just using a helper as shown in the next step.

1. When you are done with the previous steps, replace the `Index.cshtml` code as shown in the following code:

```
@foreach (var item in Model) {
    <tr>
        <td>
            @Html.DisplayFor(modelItem => item.Title)
        </td>
        <td>
            @Html.DisplayFor(modelItem => item.Description)
        </td>
        <td>
            @Html.DisplayFor(modelItem => item.IsDone)
        </td>
        <td>
            @Html.ActionLink("Edit", "Edit", new { id=item.ToDoId }) |
            @Html.ActionLink("Details", "Details", new { id=item.ToDoId }) |
            @Html.ActionLink("Delete", "Delete", new { id=item.ToDoId })
        </td>
    </tr>
}
</table>
```

```
@Html.Partial("_ToDoList", item)
```

Here, I'm rendering the partial view using the `Partial` helper method, and for each item in the model, the `Partial` helper will return a row.

RenderPartial

This helper is used to render the specified partial view by using the specified HTML helper. Also, it is very easy to use and does not need to create any action.

To explore this, let's add a fresh partial view in the Shared folder by the name of `_WelcomeNote` and write a message. Now, this partial view can be rendered on the view page using either `Partial` or `RenderPartial`, as shown in the following screenshot:

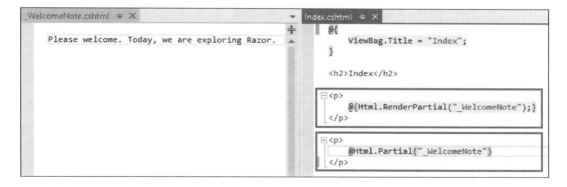

On running the application, you will see the following output:

You can see how easy it is to render a partial view using `Partial` and `RenderPartial` helper methods.

Action and RenderAction helpers

The `Action` helper is used to invoke the specified child action method that returns the result as an HTML string, whereas the `RenderAction` helper is used to invoke the specified child action method using the specified controller name and renders the result inline in the parent view. For these helpers, we need to create a child action for rendering the partial view.

To explore this, let's add a child action and update the view page, as shown in the following screenshot:

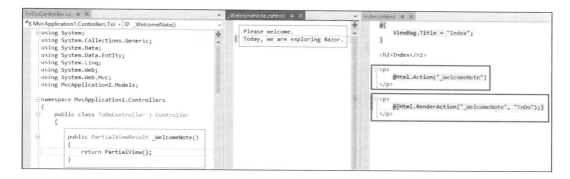

On running the application, you will see the following output:

Again, this is also very easy.

You learned various ways (`Partial`, `RenderPartial`, `Action`, and `RenderAction`) for rendering a partial view. I hope you are now quite confident with partial views and how to render them.

How it works...

By looking at these examples, you will have noticed that it is very easy to bring partial views on view page using `Partial` and `RenderPartial` helpers rather than `Action` and `RenderAction` helpers, because `Action` and `RenderAction` helpers render the partial view with the help of the controller's method (also known as the child action). So, if you just want to render a partial view, use `Partial` or `RenderPartial`, and if you want to render a partial view that accepts the model, then you need the child action returning the model.

There's more...

We can also use jQuery to make an Ajax request and load a partial view into a view. For example:

```
$('#profile').load('/account/profile');
```

Here, `#profile` is an HTML element on the view page and `account/profile` is the controller and action result respectively.

Thank you for buying
Instant Razor View Engine How-to

About Packt Publishing

Packt, pronounced 'packed', published its first book "*Mastering phpMyAdmin for Effective MySQL Management*" in April 2004 and subsequently continued to specialize in publishing highly focused books on specific technologies and solutions.

Our books and publications share the experiences of your fellow IT professionals in adapting and customizing today's systems, applications, and frameworks. Our solution based books give you the knowledge and power to customize the software and technologies you're using to get the job done. Packt books are more specific and less general than the IT books you have seen in the past. Our unique business model allows us to bring you more focused information, giving you more of what you need to know, and less of what you don't.

Packt is a modern, yet unique publishing company, which focuses on producing quality, cutting-edge books for communities of developers, administrators, and newbies alike. For more information, please visit our website: www.packtpub.com.

Writing for Packt

We welcome all inquiries from people who are interested in authoring. Book proposals should be sent to author@packtpub.com. If your book idea is still at an early stage and you would like to discuss it first before writing a formal book proposal, contact us; one of our commissioning editors will get in touch with you.

We're not just looking for published authors; if you have strong technical skills but no writing experience, our experienced editors can help you develop a writing career, or simply get some additional reward for your expertise.

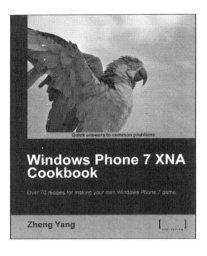

Windows Phone 7 XNA Cookbook

ISBN: 978-1-84969-120-8   Paperback: 450 pages

Over 70 recipes for making your own Windows Phone 7 game

1. Complete focus on the best Windows Phone 7 game development techniques using XNA 4.0

2. Easy to follow cookbook allowing you to dive in wherever you want.

3. Convert ideas into action using practical recipes

Instant Creating Data Models with PowerPivot How-to

ISBN: 978-1-84968-956-4   Paperback: 58 pages

Build better business intelligence with this practical guide to creating Excel data models with PowerPivot

1. Learn something new in an Instant! A short, fast, focused guide delivering immediate results

2. Detailed, step-by-step interactive tutorial guide to learning PowerPivot

3. Carefully organized topics for users of all levels

4. Learn how to make your data accessible and attractive

Please check **www.PacktPub.com** for information on our titles

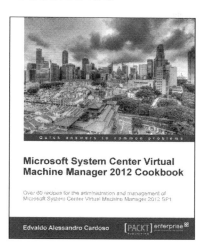

Microsoft System Center Virtual
Machine Manager 2012 Cookbook

Over 60 recipes for the administration and management of
Microsoft System Center Virtual Machine Manager 2012 SP1

Edvaldo Alessandro Cardoso   [PACKT] enterprise

Microsoft System Center Virtual Machine Manager 2012 Cookbook

ISBN: 978-1-84968-632-7   Paperback: 342 pages

Over 60 recipes for the administration and management of Microsoft System Center Virtual Machine Manager 2012 SP1

1. Create, deploy, and manage Datacentres, Private and Hybrid Clouds with hybrid hypervisors by using VMM 2012 SP1, App Controller, and Operations Manager.

2. Integrate and manage fabric (compute, storages, gateways, networking) services and resources. Deploy Clusters from bare metal servers.

3. Learn how to use VMM 2012 SP1 features such as Windows 2012 and SQL 2012 support, Network Virtualization, Live Migration, Linux VMs, Resource Throttling, and Availability.

Microsoft Visual C++
Windows Applications by Example

Code and explanation for real-world MFC C++ Applications

Stefan Björnander   [PACKT]

Microsoft Visual C++ Windows Applications by Example

ISBN: 978-1-84719-556-2   Paperback: 440 pages

Code and explanation for real-world MFC C++ Applications

1. Learn C++ Windows programming by studying realistic, interesting examples

2. A quick primer in Visual C++ for programmers of other languages, followed by deep, thorough examples

3. Example applications include a Tetris-style game, a spreadsheet application, a drawing application, and a word processor

Please check **www.PacktPub.com** for information on our titles